Malcolm Arnold

Four Scottish Dances

arranged for piano

by John York

These dances were composed early in 1957 and are dedicated to the BBC Light Music Festival. They are all based on original melodies, except one, the melody of which was composed by Robert Burns.

The first dance is in the style of a slow strathspey.

The second, a lively reel, begins in the key of E flat, and rises a semitone each time it is played. The final statement of the dance is at the original speed in the home key of E flat.

The third dance is in the style of a Hebridean song and attempts to give an impression of the sea and mountain scenery on a calm summer's day in the Hebrides.

The last dance is a lively fling.

NOVELLO

Four Scottish Dances, Op. 59

Malcolm Arnold
arr. John York

I

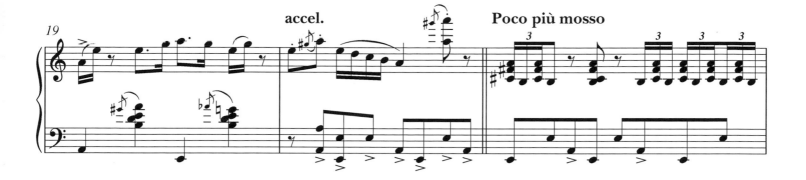

accel. Poco più mosso

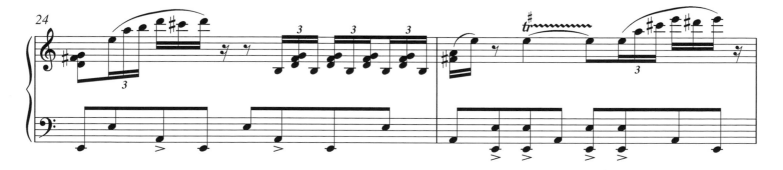

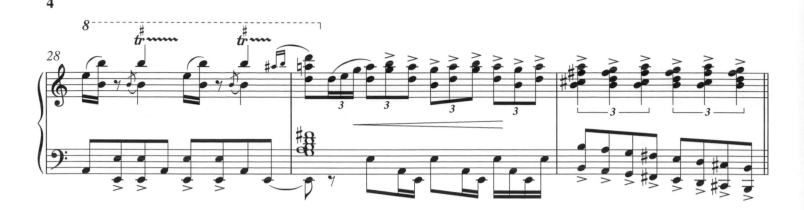

Tempo I ♩ = 104

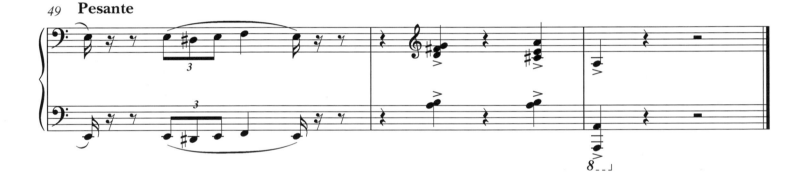

II

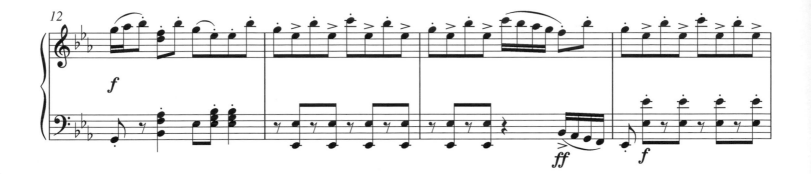

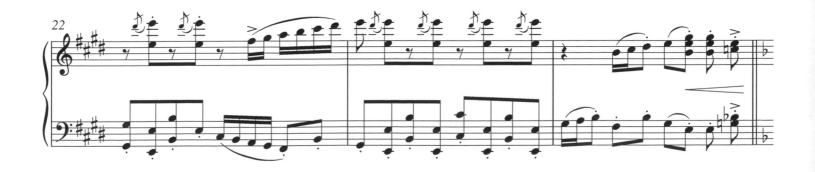

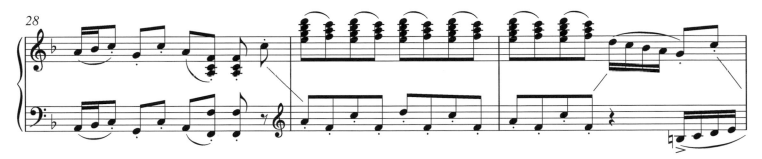

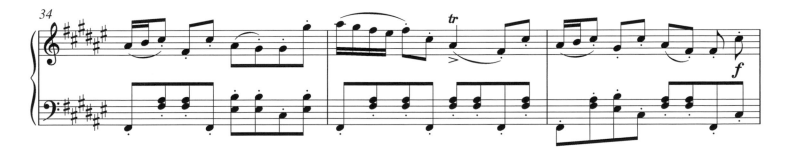

Meno mosso ♩ = 112

Tempo I (Vivace ♩ = 160)

III

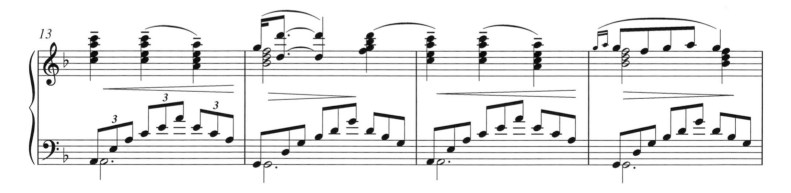

IV

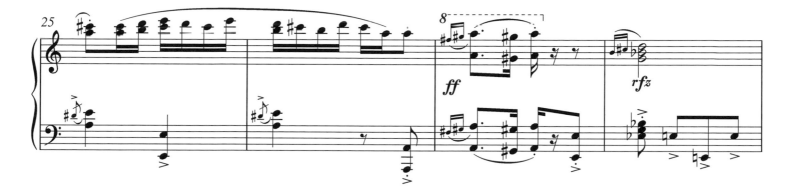

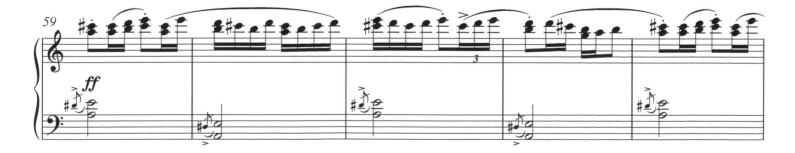

Cover design by Fresh Lemon
Music setting by Jack Thompson

Order no. NOV121143
ISBN 1-84449-317-2

Head office:
8/9 Frith Street, London W1D 3JB
Tel. +44 (0)20 7434 0066
Fax +44 (0)20 7287 6329

Sales and Hire:
Music Sales Distribution Centre,
Newmarket Road, Bury St Edmunds, Suffolk IP33 3YB
Tel. +44 (0)1284 702600
Fax +44 (0)1284 768301

www.chesternovello.com
e-mail: music@musicsales.co.uk